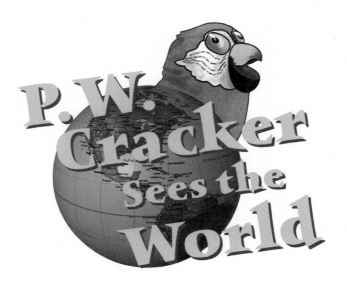

P.W. Cracker Sees the World

Written by Linda Yoshizawa
Illustrated by Eric Berendt

STECK-VAUGHN
ELEMENTARY · SECONDARY · ADULT · LIBRARY

A Harcourt Classroom Education Company

www.steck-vaughn.com

Contents

Chapter One

Have Dream, Will Travel

"**S**ettle down, everyone," Mrs. Carter told her students. "It's time for our geography lesson." Chairs scraped, papers rustled, and pencils tapped.

P.W. Cracker, the class parrot, clicked his beak loudly. Twenty-four heads turned to look at him. P.W. stood up straight on his perch. "Settle down, everyone!" he said in a clear voice.

The students giggled and then quieted down. "Thank you, P.W.," Mrs. Carter said with a smile.

P.W. bobbed his head up and down. He liked being in Mrs. Carter's class. It was much better than living with all those noisy little parakeets at the pet store. P.W. knew there was more to life than climbing a little ladder and trying to peck the bird in the mirror.

P.W. had learned a lot in Mrs. Carter's class. He'd memorized the multiplication tables and knew how to write a letter. He could spell *Mississippi* and read poetry. But the subject he loved most was geography. Every time the class studied a new country, P.W. forgot about preening his feathers. He didn't even think about watching the sparrows outside. Instead, he dreamed of visiting faraway lands.

"It's time to share our geography projects," Mrs. Carter said to the class. She pulled down the map of the world. "Who wants to go first?"

"Who wants to go first?" P.W. repeated. He had been looking forward to this day all week.

Mei raised her hand. "This summer my cousin from China visited us," she said. "I took him to a baseball game. He taught me to eat with chopsticks." Mei picked up a pair of chopsticks from her desk. She showed the class how to hold them to eat.

P.W. flew over and perched on Mei's shoulder. *Wow! Eating with sticks! Much better than using claws*, he thought.

Next, Juan shared his project. It was a small statue of a strange-looking creature. "My aunt works in Egypt. She sent me this model of the Great Sphinx in the mail," Juan told the rest of the class.

"Sphinx in the mail," P.W. said. He flew over to Juan's desk. Cocking his head, he stared at the statue. *This sphinx thing is really something*, he said to himself. *The head looks like a man's, but I think the body is a lion's.*

As the other students shared their projects, P.W. fluttered to their desks and bobbed his head excitedly. By the end of the geography lesson, his head was spinning.

The class went on to their math lesson. They learned about triangles. P.W. thought about China. Then the class went on to spelling. P.W.'s mind was on England. He got so excited about a real palace with a real queen that he couldn't even think about how to spell *disappear*.

When the students left for the day, P.W. flew over to the map. Perched on the chalkboard ledge, he stared at the world.

"I love learning about all these countries," P.W. said aloud. "England, France, Egypt, China, Panama. What an adventure it would be to visit every one them!" Then an idea popped into P.W.'s head. "That's what I'll do!" he decided. "I'll go to the places we've studied. My trip will be the best geography project ever! P.W. Cracker is off to see the world!"

Excited about his plan, P.W. flapped his wings. When Mrs. Carter left for the day, he searched the class lost-and-found box. He found a little backpack. He borrowed the instant camera that the class used for field trips. Into the backpack went the camera. Next, P.W. took some paper, envelopes, and some markers from Mrs. Carter's desk. He stuffed them in the backpack, too. Then he wrote a note to Mrs. Carter and the class.

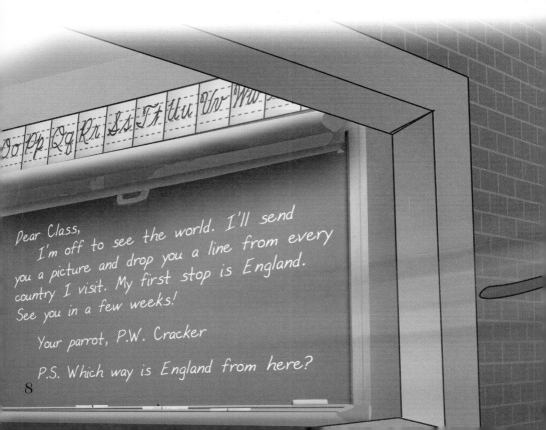

Dear Class,

I'm off to see the world. I'll send you a picture and drop you a line from every country I visit. My first stop is England. See you in a few weeks!

Your parrot, P.W. Cracker

P.S. Which way is England from here?

P.W. slung the backpack over a wing. Then he hopped to the window. Using his strong beak, he turned the latch. Cr-r-r-eak! The window opened.

Outside, the wind ruffled P.W.'s tail feathers. The sun warmed his wings. "Get ready, big wide world!" he called as he flew into the blue sky. "Here I come!"

Chapter Two

English Rocks

"**N**ow this is what being a parrot is all about," P.W. said as he zoomed away from the school. It was great to go just as fast as he wanted. Soon he was far away. He flew over a shopping mall. He flew over houses, trees, more houses, and more trees. His wings began to ache. He fluttered to a stop on top of a billboard.

"Whew!" P.W. wheezed. "The world is a lot bigger than I realized. Maybe I'm not strong enough to fly to England."

P.W. heard a roaring sound overhead. He looked up. An airplane was about to land at the airport. "Boy, they sure can fly fast," he observed, "a lot faster than a bird." Then an idea hit him. "An airplane! I'll hop on a plane and fly to England. No more aching wings for me!"

At the airport P.W. landed on top of a parked taxicab. He scratched his head with a claw and wondered how to find a plane going to England. He was preening a stray wing feather when the taxicab door opened. A woman with silver hair and a straw hat got out. Colorful fruit decorated the top of her hat.

Dinner! P.W. said to himself and hopped into the fruit. He bit into a grape hungrily. *Yuck!* He spat out bits of green plastic as the woman walked up to a man at an airport door.

"Which airline, ma'am?" the man asked the woman. P.W. didn't hear what the woman said. He was busy getting the last bit of plastic unstuck from his beak.

"Which flight?" the man asked.

"Number 348, to England," the woman replied.

"Better hurry," the man advised her.

England! P.W.'s feathers perked up. He was in luck! "Number 348, to—" he began to repeat. Then he saw the man look hard at the hat. P.W. slapped a wing over his beak. If the man knew he was a real parrot, the man might try to catch him. This was no time to talk. P.W. froze next to an orange. The woman walked into the airport.

P.W. held tight to a banana as the woman hurried to her plane. When she finally reached her seat, P.W. sighed happily. He didn't get dinner, but at least he didn't have to fly to England with his own two wings.

The woman took off her hat and placed it in the luggage rack. P.W. nestled among the fruit. He closed his eyes and tucked his head under a wing. England was thousands of miles away. It would be a l-o-o-o-ng flight.

When P.W. woke up, he was still on the hat, but he and the hat were in a hotel room. It was daylight outside. *Where am I?* he wondered.

How long have I been asleep? I must have had a bad case of jet lag. Just then he saw the woman heading straight for the hat. He froze. She put her hat on.

Outside the hotel, the woman headed for a tour bus. P.W. shivered in the cool, wet air. "See Stonehenge" was written in giant letters on the side of the bus. P.W. decided to see what a Stonehenge was.

The bus drove through the crowded streets of London, then into the country. Through a light fog, P.W. saw green fields all around. A light drizzle beaded the windows of the bus.

When the bus stopped, P.W. flew out a window. He soared into the sky. Then he looked down and saw a giant ring of rocks. The sight took his breath away. He had to find out more about this Stonehenge place.

An English sparrow flew up beside P.W. "Care for a tour, old chap?" he asked.

"I sure would," P.W. answered. "And would you take a picture of me? I want to send it back home."

"Happy to oblige."

P.W. landed on top of one of the stones. The sparrow snapped a photo of him. Then he told P.W. all about Stonehenge. When the bus headed back to London, P.W. settled under a seat and wrote a letter to the class.

From the perch of
P.W. Cracker

Dear Class,

Here I am in England at Stonehenge. These rocks are HUGE!

A sparrow here says that people began building Stonehenge 5,000 years ago. First they dug a ditch with tools made from deer antlers and wood. Later they dragged the stones into circles. Some of the stones came from a mountain range over 200 miles away.

No one knows for sure why Stonehenge was built or what it was used for. Maybe we can figure it out when I get back!

Cheerio, chaps! I'm off to see a tower almost as tall as the Empire State Building. Bet you can't guess where it is!

A little cold and damp,
P.W. Cracker

P.S. Do they make umbrellas for parrots?

Chapter Three

Long Live France!

Back in London, P.W. mailed his letter and perched close to the hotel entrance. He was cold and tired after his day. He was also wondering how he was going to get to France, when he heard a woman say "Merci." From geography class he knew that was French for "thank you." Maybe the woman was from France. Maybe she was going home! "Merci!" P.W. repeated.

The woman kept talking in French. With his eagle eye, P.W. saw that the woman was young, and she held a baby. On the sidewalk beside her sat a huge bag filled with diapers and baby bottles and baby toys. It looked full, but it was open at the top. P.W. went for it. First he glided silently down to the sidewalk. Then he pecked around on the ground. When no one was looking, he slipped into the baby's bag.

The woman got on a bus that took them to a train station. P.W. knew he had to cross the English Channel to get to France. *Does the train turn into a boat?* he wondered.

On the train, the woman sat down and held the baby in her arms. She set the bag with P.W. in it next to her. A man sat on P.W.'s other side. He had a cat in a cage. P.W. peeped out of the baby's bag. He peered into the cage. "Excuse me, does this train float?" he whispered to the cat.

The cat meowed in laughter. "No! The train travels through a tunnel built under the English Channel. The tunnel is called the Chunnel."

P.W.'s beak dropped. They were traveling UNDER the water? He was so shocked that he almost meowed, too.

Being underwater made P.W. nervous. He was also hungry. He fished around in the baby bag for something to eat. At the bottom of it, he found something in a plastic wrapper. *It might be a cracker,* he thought. He bit through the wrapper. "Blechh!" he squawked aloud. "A baby biscuit!" he whispered loudly to himself. "No wonder babies just play with these things. I'm starving, and it still tastes weird."

P.W. spat the biscuit out and peeped out of the bag again. *Please let me get to France soon,* he wished. *I hear French food is wonderful.*

The train finally reached France at dusk. Too tired to try to find any French food, P.W. parked himself in a tree, tucked his head under his wing, and went to sleep.

The next morning P.W. found some people tossing out food for the pigeons. He grabbed a quick breakfast and waited in a tree by the road to Paris. At last a man in a truck came along. P.W. darted into the back of the truck. He spent the rest of the morning among baskets of mushrooms. Still hungry, he tried one. He decided it was even worse than the baby biscuit.

By noon P.W. had reached Paris, and he was starving. Along a river he saw a French poodle that looked friendly. He trotted up to the dog. "Excuse me," he said politely. "Do you know where I can find a good meal around here?"

"Oui," the poodle replied.

"No, me," said P.W. "But you can come if you want to."

The poodle gave a sniff. "Silly parrot," he said. "*Oui* only sounds like *we*. In French, *oui* means 'yes.' Try the little café on the corner just ahead."

An hour later a very full P.W. flew back to the riverbank. The poodle was still there.

"The French bread is very good at the café, no?" asked the poodle.

"Oui!" replied P.W.

After lunch P.W. looked around for the Eiffel Tower. Rising almost 1,000 feet in the air, it was easy to spot. P.W. soared to the top for a good look at Paris.

On the way down, P.W. met a friendly pigeon who agreed to take his picture. Click! He had a photo to send home.

From the perch of
P.W. Cracker

Dear Class,

Here I am, perched on the famous Eiffel Tower. It was built in 1889 for a world's fair and is made of iron and steel. Back then, steel was a new kind of building material. For a while, the Eiffel Tower was the tallest building in the world.

The Eiffel tower was named for the man who built it. He's the same person who designed the frame inside the Statue of Liberty in New York.

My third stop will take me to one of the Seven Wonders of the Ancient World. Can you guess where I'm going?

Oui, I am still your parrot,
P.W. Cracker

P.S. These French people really know how to make bread!

P.W. spent the night on the Eiffel Tower. The next morning he flew to a mailbox to mail his letter. He spotted two young men on motorbikes. P.W. listened to them carefully. They were speaking French, so he couldn't understand a lot of what they were saying. He did figure out that their names were Julian and Robert. Then he heard Julian say "Egypt."

Egypt! Maybe they're going there, P.W. thought. *Maybe I can hop a ride with them.*

P.W. flew down and perched on the handlebars of Julian's bike. "Egypt," he repeated. He gave Julian his best parrot smile and bobbed his head up and down.

Julian laughed and said something else in French to Robert. Then he started his engine, and the three headed off.

23

Chapter Four

A View from a Sphinx

It took the three a day to travel through France. Finally Julian, Robert, and P.W. reached a city in the southern part of the country. It was late, and P.W. was sleepy and windblown.

P.W. spent the night on the handlebars of Julian's motorbike. The next day, his two friends pushed their bikes onto a ferry. P.W. flew onto the top deck and perched on the railing.

The ferry chugged into the Mediterranean Sea. Crystal-blue water sparkled. Sun-baked rocks stuck out of the water. Damp, salty air sprayed P.W.'s feathers. *It's amazing how a good bath can make you feel like a new parrot,* he thought. He preened his windblown feathers and ate some trail mix that Julian gave him. He was ready for Egypt.

They passed the coasts of Italy, Greece, and Turkey. Finally the boat docked at a port in Egypt. From there P.W. rode with Julian and Robert to Cairo, the huge city on the Nile River. The crowded streets were hot and dusty. P.W. would have loved another bath. But the Nile looked too brown and muddy.

As Julian's bike swerved through traffic, P.W. studied the people. Women wore long dresses. A few men wore long robes. *How do they wear all those long clothes when it's so hot here?* he wondered. Just looking at the people made him hot, so he spread his wings to cool off.

When they stopped in the town of Giza, P.W. hopped onto Julian's shoulder. Then he saw something that almost made him jump out of his feathers. Above him towered a huge statue. It was the man with the lion's body!

P.W. bobbed his head up and down. "Sphinx!" he said aloud.

"The Great Sphinx of Giza," said a nearby pair of camels. P.W. fluttered over to one of them and set up the camera on its hump. Then he hopped over to the other and posed. Click! He wanted to go for a camel ride, but the camels were not very friendly. So P.W. flew into the clouds to get a bird's-eye view of Giza. He sailed around the sphinx's face and saw that it had been worn away by wind and rain. Then he flew the length of the body. It was about as long as a football field.

Hot and tired, P.W. perched on top of a nearby pyramid. Whoa! Now he was really high! To the west lay the desert. Below him, tourists waited in line for a camel ride. He couldn't wait to tell the class all about Egypt. Pulling a sheet of paper from his backpack, P.W. started to write.

From the perch of
P.W. Cracker

Dear Class,

I'm writing to you from the top of a pyramid. That's right. I'm 446 feet in the air! A pyramid is a tomb where an Egyptian king was buried. One pyramid here was made from more than 2 million stone blocks!

The huge statue in the picture is the Great Sphinx. It was carved out of stone and has the face of a king. For a long time the Great Sphinx was buried in the sand. Then a prince had a dream. The dream said he would become a king if he cleared away the sand.

Next I'm off to see something much bigger than a pyramid. I'll bet you can't guess what it is!

Your sun-baked parrot,
P.W. Cracker

P.S. Did you know camels can spit?

Chapter Five

Along a Great Wall

P.W. flew the letter back into Cairo, mailed it, and headed for the airport. He was now an expert at catching rides, so he looked for just the right man outside the airport. He unzipped a pocket on the man's luggage and slipped in. Soon he was on a plane going east.

The next day P.W. stared down at a crowded street in Beijing, China. He was hungry again. He didn't see any other birds around, but there were lots of people and lots of noise and lots of apartment buildings. "This place sure is hard to get around in!" P.W. said as he flew down another street lined with apartments.

He was so busy trying to figure out how to get out of the city that he didn't watch where he was going. Splat!

P.W. flew right
into a window and
tumbled down into a
booth. He struggled to
his feet and popped up
for a look. All around
were other booths with
different kinds of foods.
Across the street he saw cabbages
and pretty little oranges. Next to him was a
booth filled with fish of all kinds for sale, even
squid.

I must be at some kind of food market, P.W.
decided. He walked along the edge of his booth.
There were some things hanging above him. Their
shape looked familiar.

P.W. heard a little clucking sound and walked
a little farther. Looking down, he saw a chicken
in a cage. *I think I'll go down and say hello,* P.W.
thought to himself. *I wonder why he's in that ca—.*

In that instant P.W. figured out what the
hanging things were. "AGGHHHH!" he squawked.
He didn't know if Chinese people liked to eat

parrots, but he wasn't taking any chances. He blasted out of the booth like a red rocket and didn't stop until he had found the edge of the city. He spent the rest of the day with his head under his wing.

The next morning P.W.'s courage returned. He flew northward for the rest of that day and all of the next. He had to stop and rest often, but his wings got much stronger. He looked for a café where he might have some French bread. Instead, he found delicious noodles and rice.

At last P.W. stared down at the awesome sight he was looking for—the Great Wall of China! It stretched as far as he could see, winding across the lush, green mountains like a snake.

P.W. landed on top of a stone watchtower. "The wall was built to protect China from enemy armies," someone said. P.W. glanced around. A squirrel scampered up and sat beside him.

"If a soldier saw an attacking army, he would signal the other soldiers," the squirrel told P.W. "He would shoot off a cannon. One blast meant one thousand soldiers. More cannon blasts meant more soldiers."

"More soldiers," P.W. repeated. He could almost hear the roar of the cannons. "Wait until I tell the class back home," he told the squirrel. Then he pulled out his camera. "Would you take a picture of me?" he asked.

"Sure." The squirrel took P.W.'s picture. Then he scampered off to get a treat from a tourist. P.W. wrote a letter to the class.

From the perch of
P.W. Cracker

Dear Class,

Here I am on the Great Wall of China. They call it "great" because it's 4,000 miles long. It would stretch across the United States. Thousands of men spent 100 years building it.

Next time I write, I'll be closer to the United States. That's the only clue I'm going to give you.

Your parrot,
P.W. Cracker

P.S. Rice sure does stick to a parrot's beak!

Chapter Six

From the Pacific to the Atlantic

Now that his wings were strong, P.W. flew and flew across China. Finally he reached the busy port of Hong Kong. The port was filled with all kinds of ships, from yachts and cruise ships to working freighters.

P.W. was tired from all the traveling he had done. He circled above a freighter. Cranes were loading huge wooden boxes onto the deck. The boxes had *Panama* written on the sides.

All right! P.W. thought. *That's the country I want to visit next.* He flew down to the deck, settled into a nest of rope, and fell fast asleep.

When P.W. woke up, the ship was moving. He flew to the top of a pole and looked around. The freighter was in the middle of the Pacific Ocean. All P.W. could see was sky and water.

A few days later, the ship neared land. "Land ho!" cried a sailor.

"Land ho!" echoed P.W.

"It must be Central America," a sailor yelled back. "We're headed for the Panama Canal!"

"Panama Canal!" repeated P.W. excitedly. He remembered from a geography lesson that the canal was a waterway through the country of Panama. It connected the Pacific and the Atlantic oceans. Because the oceans were not on the same level, ships had to go through locks. The locks filled up with water, raised the ship, and then let the water out.

P.W. flapped his wings nervously as his freighter entered the first lock. The gate closed. The lock filled with water. When the ship was at the right level, the front gate opened, and the ship sailed on toward the next lock.

P.W. flew to the lock ahead. While he wrote his letter, he thought about the workers who built the canal. It had taken them ten years to build it. Many had died as they carved the canal out of solid rock and dense rain forest. Even now the rain forest grew right next to the canal in many places. P.W. waved to red and green parrots along the shore. He feasted on fresh fruit from the jungle. And once he heard the scream of a jaguar.

From the perch of P.W. Cracker

Dear Class,

Did you guess where I am? The Panama Canal's really cool. Actually, it's hot except when a sudden storm blows over. It rains hard, then the sun comes out. Everything gets steamy. It makes a parrot feel right at home.

It's a good thing President Theodore Roosevelt decided to have the canal built. Otherwise, my ship would have to sail all the way around South America to get home. Going through the canal shortens the trip by 7,000 miles.

By the time you get this letter, I'll probably be home.

Your parrot, the sailor,
P.W. Cracker

P.S. Do jaguars eat parrots?

Chapter Seven

Home, Sweet Home

When the freighter reached the end of the canal, P.W. cheered. At the airport in Panama, he found an American woman going to his home city. He hopped in her purse.

"Ahh," P.W. sighed as he kicked back among the lipsticks and chewing gum. He closed his eyes. Soon he'd see his friends again.

When the plane landed at lunchtime, P.W. headed for the school. He had one more picture to take. He hopped up the school steps. He posed beside the front door. Snap! He took his last shot.

P.W. circled around the school until a teacher opened the front door. He zoomed down the halls to Mrs. Carter's room. There he found a surprise. A big banner was stretched above the map. It said, "Welcome Home, P.W.!" Each of his pictures was taped to the map.

P.W. taped his last picture to the display as the bell for lunch to end rang. He could hear the kids chattering as they came down the halls.

Excited and tired, P.W walked back and forth on his perch. *I can't wait to see them!* he thought, ruffling his feathers excitedly. *I'm so glad to be back home.*

Then he glanced at the map. He thought about all the places he'd been and all the good food he'd eaten. His eyelids drooped. Before the class entered the room, P.W.'s head was tucked under his wing.

When the children came in, they gathered around P.W., wondering why he was fast asleep in the middle of the day. They didn't know he was dreaming of plastic grapes and baby biscuits, French bread, trail mix, noodles, and rice. . . .